easy piano

Happy Birthday to You, Heart and Soul

AND OTHER GREAT SONGS

ISBN 978-1-4803-4435-8

HAL•LEONARD®
CORPORATION

7777 W. BLUEMOUND RD. P.O. BOX 13819 MILWAUKEE, WI 53213

Visit Hal Leonard Online at
www.halleonard.com

CHITTY CHITTY BANG BANG

Words and Music by RICHARD M. SHERMAN
and ROBERT B. SHERMAN

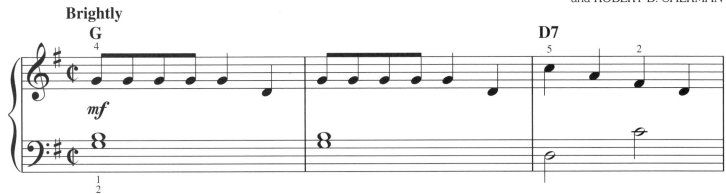

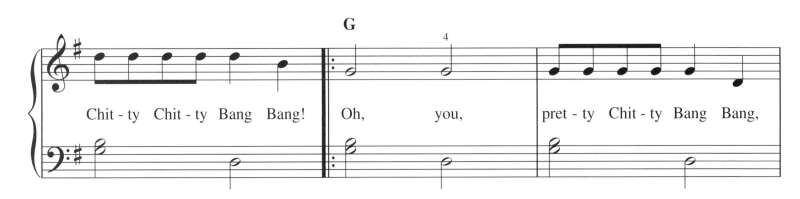

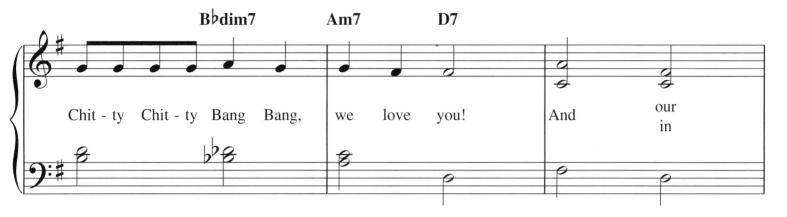

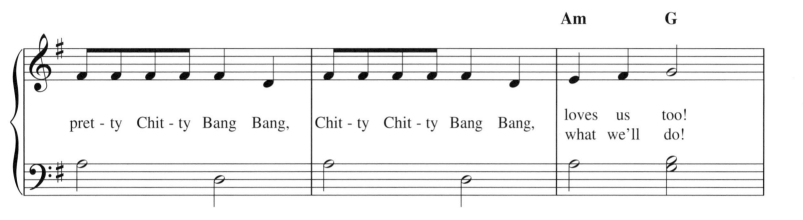

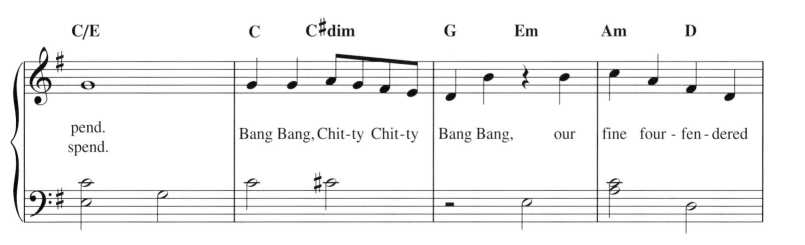

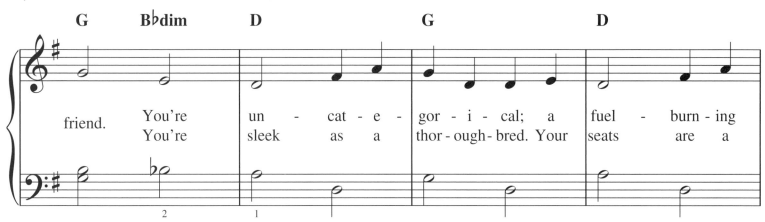

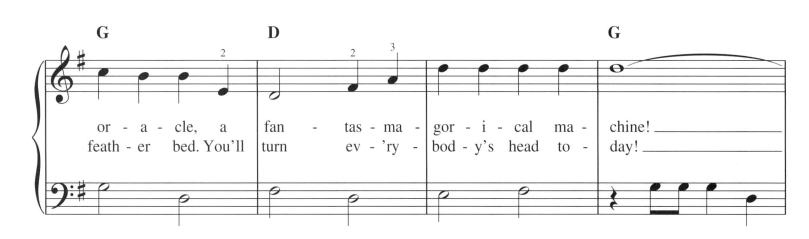

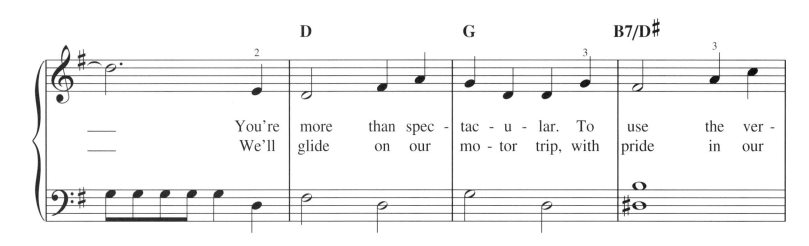

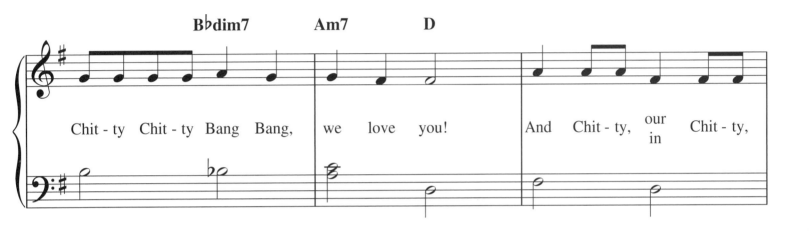

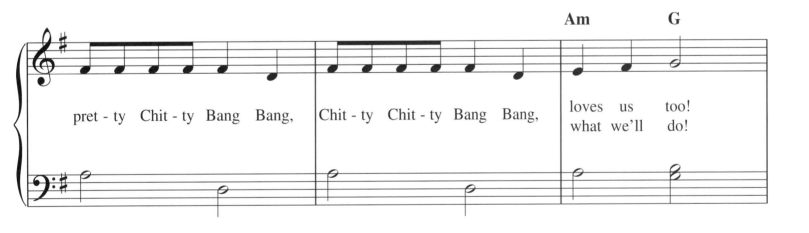

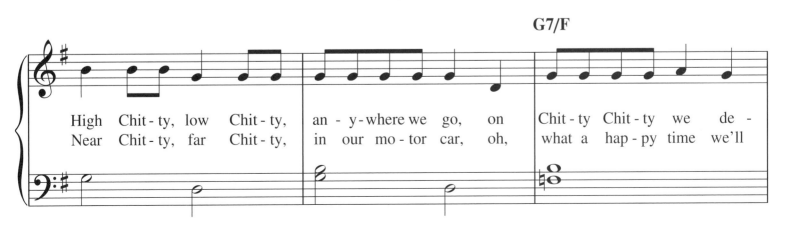

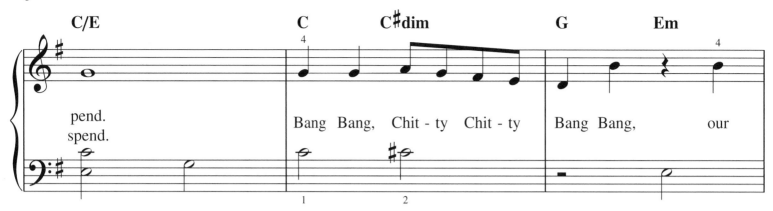

pend.
spend.

Bang Bang, Chit - ty Chit - ty   Bang Bang,   our

fine   four - fen - dered   friend!   friend!

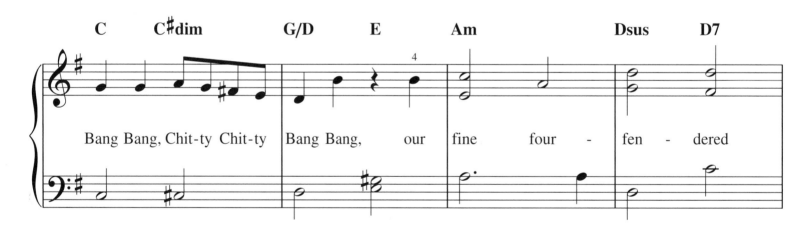

Bang Bang, Chit-ty Chit-ty   Bang Bang,   our   fine   four -   fen - dered

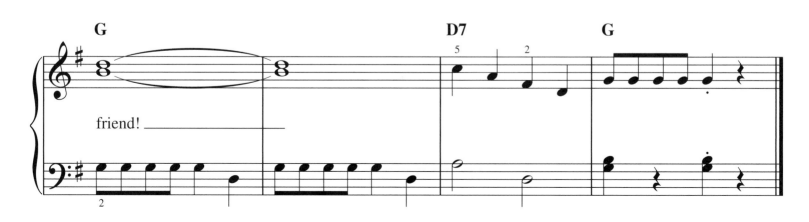

friend! _____

GOOD NIGHT

Words and Music by JOHN LENNON
and PAUL McCARTNEY

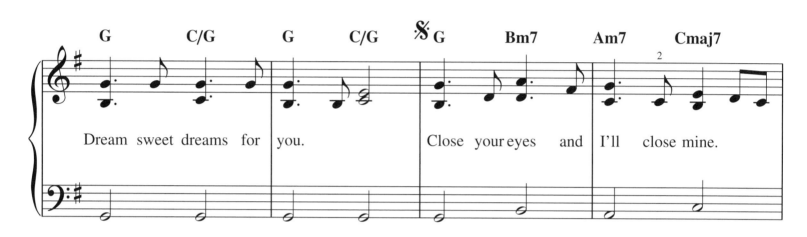

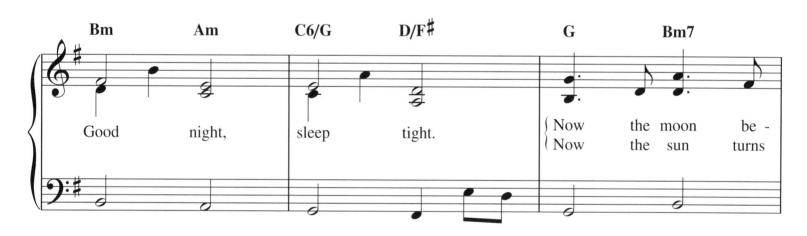

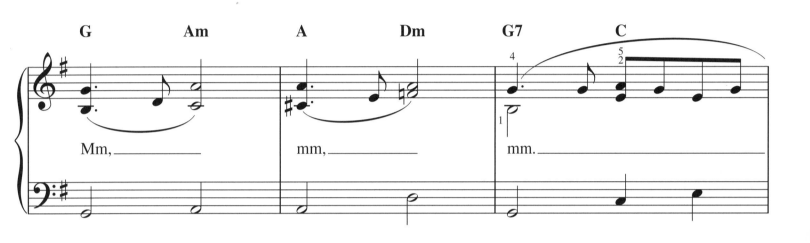

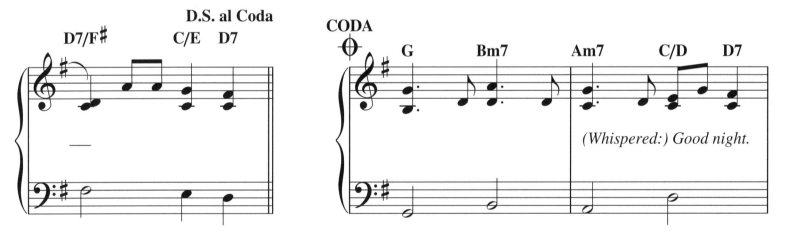

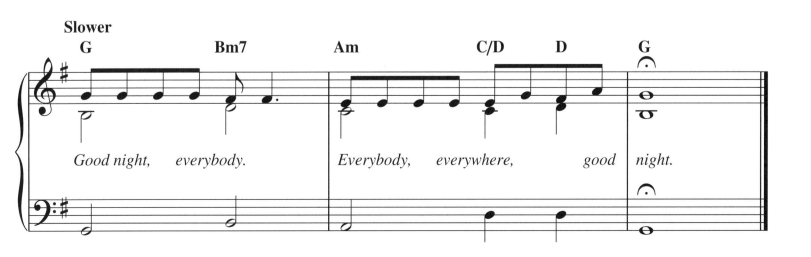

DING-DONG! THE WITCH IS DEAD
from THE WIZARD OF OZ

Lyrics by E.Y. "YIP" HARBURG
Music by HAROLD ARLEN

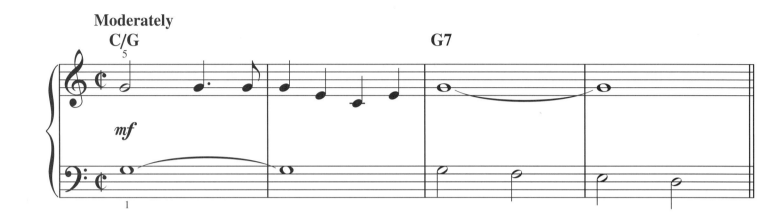

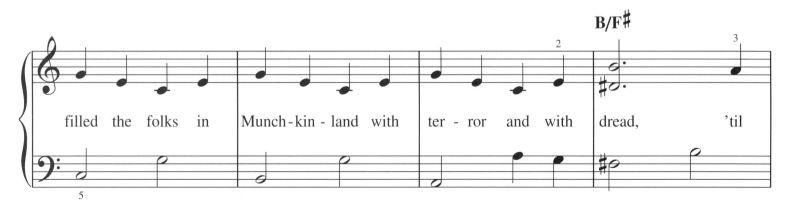

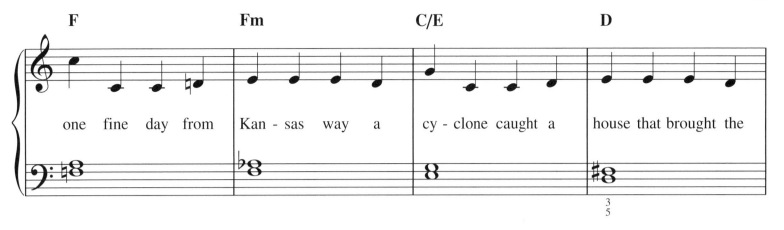

one fine day from | Kan - sas way a | cy - clone caught a | house that brought the

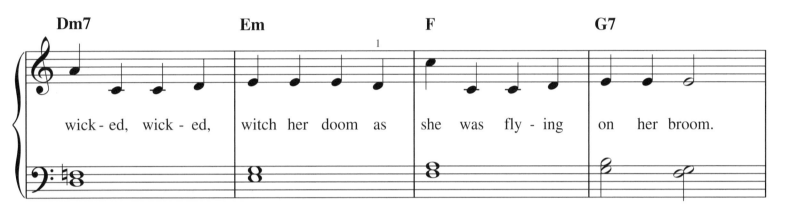

wick - ed, wick - ed, | witch her doom as | she was fly - ing | on her broom.

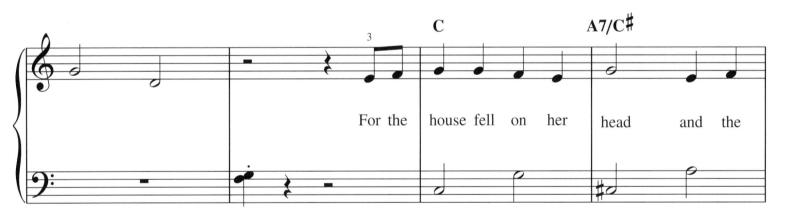

For the | house fell on her | head and the

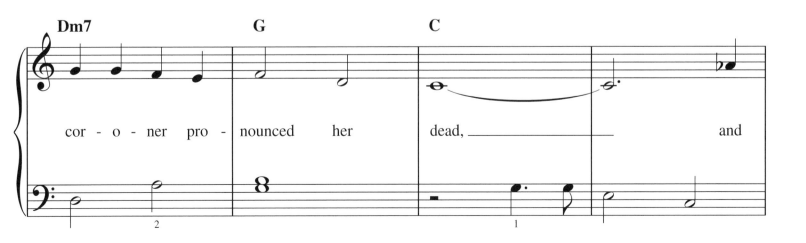

cor - o - ner pro - | nounced her | dead, _____ | and

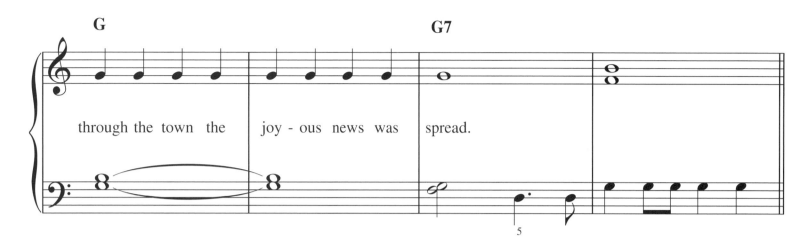

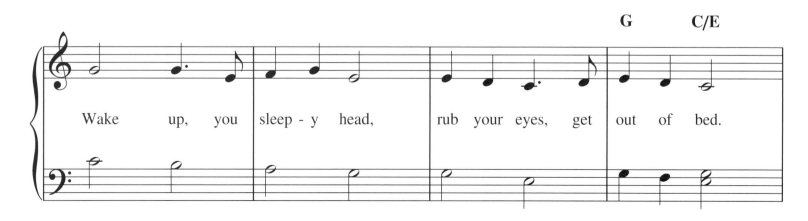

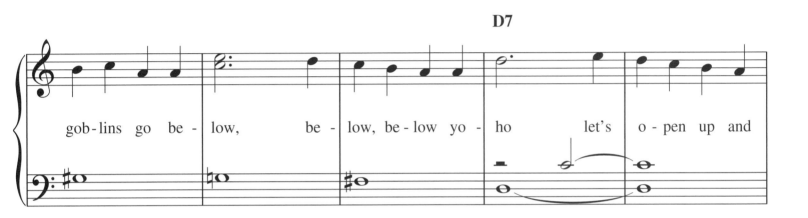

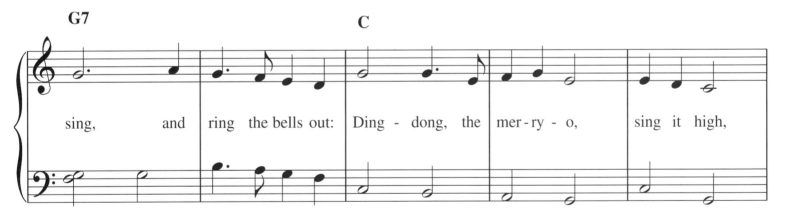

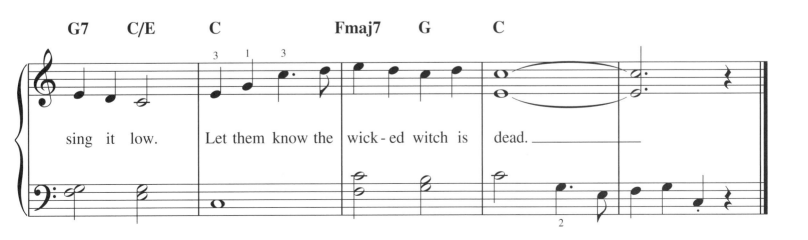

GOOFUS

Music by WAYNE KING
and WILLIAM HAROLD
Words by GUS KAHN

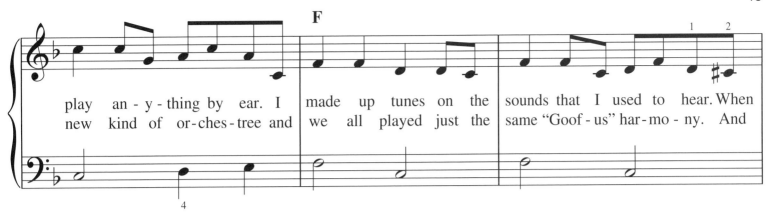

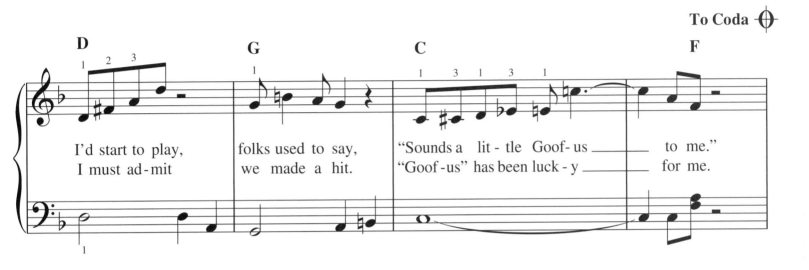

Not ac-cord-ing to the rules _ that you learn in mu-sic schools, _

D.S. al Coda

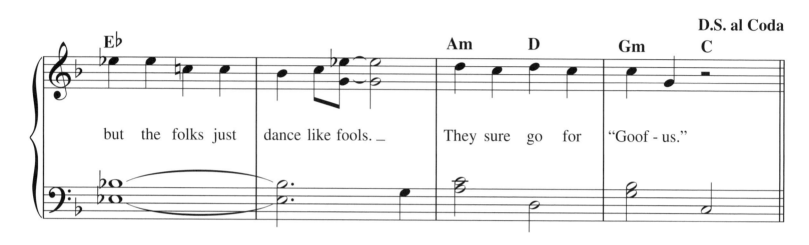

but the folks just dance like fools. _ They sure go for "Goof-us."

CODA

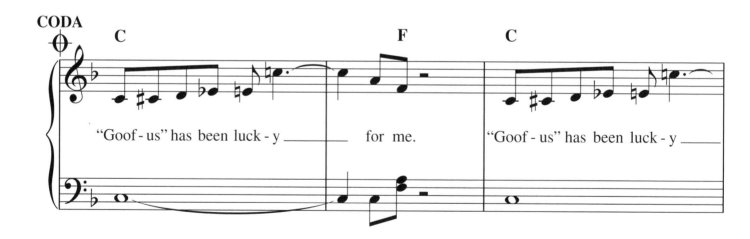

"Goof-us" has been luck-y _____ for me. "Goof-us" has been luck-y _____

for me.

HAPPY BIRTHDAY TO YOU

Words and Music by MILDRED J. HILL
and PATTY S. HILL

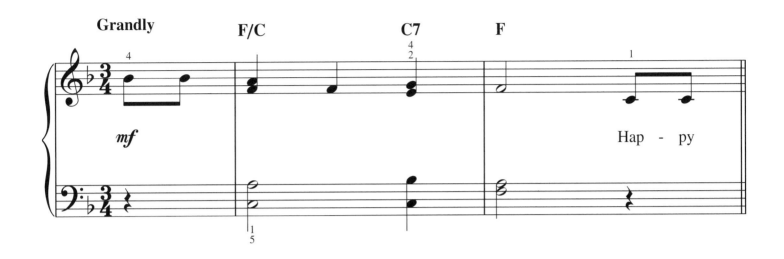

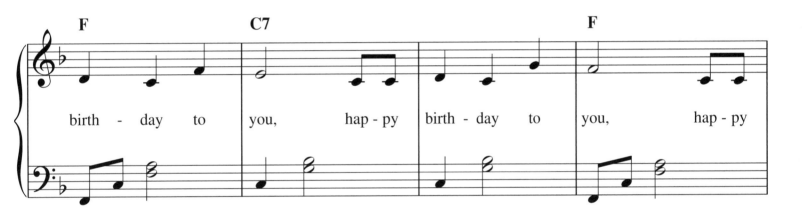

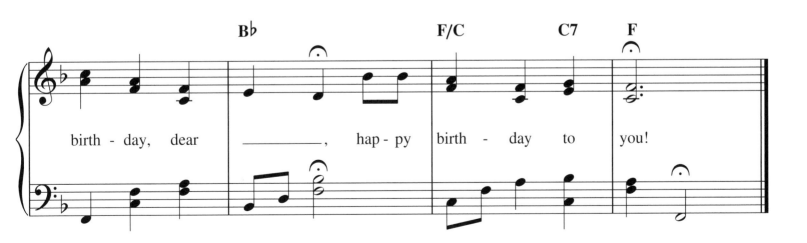

HEART AND SOUL
from the Paramount Short Subject A SONG IS BORN

Words by FRANK LOESSER
Music by HOAGY CARMICHAEL

Moderately

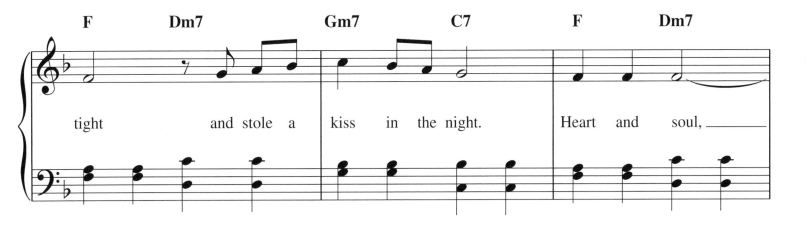

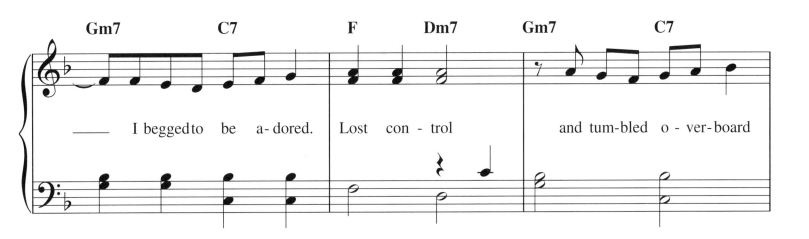

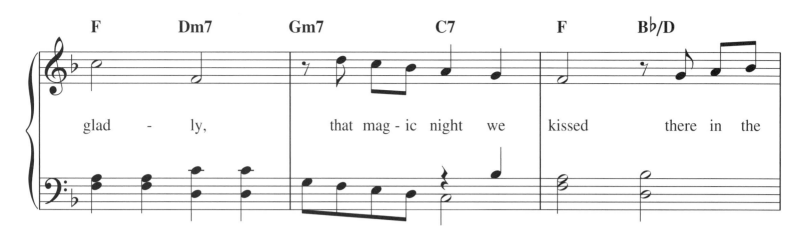

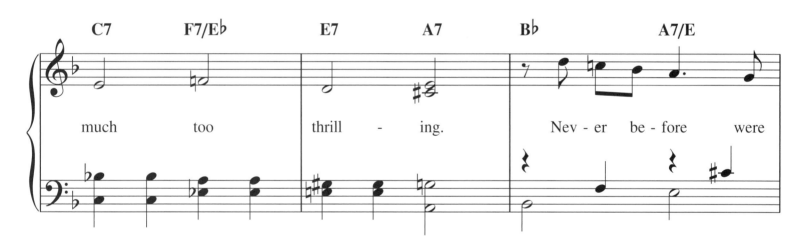

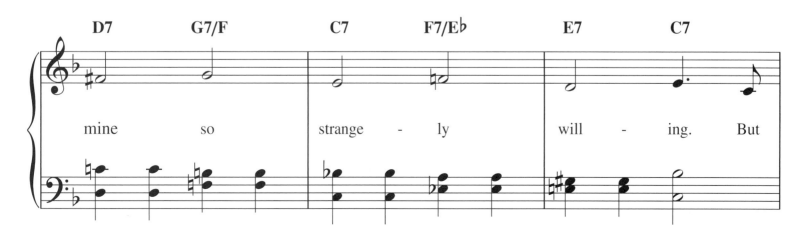

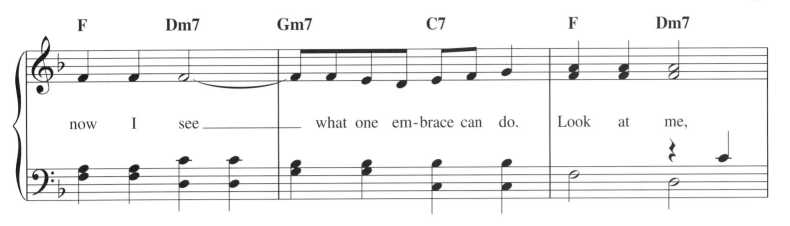

now I see _____ what one em-brace can do. Look at me,

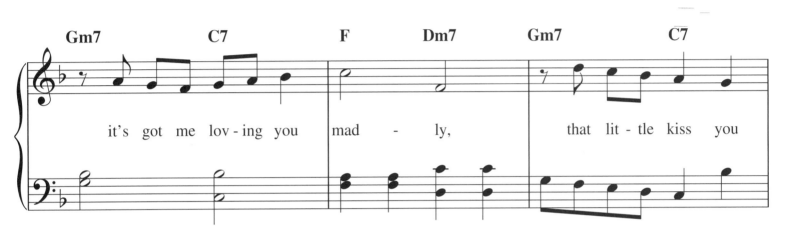

it's got me lov-ing you mad - ly, that lit - tle kiss you

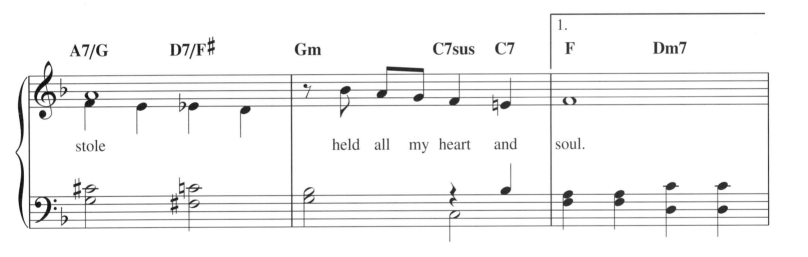

stole held all my heart and soul.

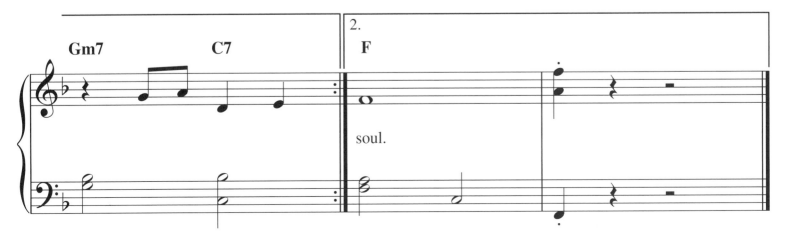

soul.

HI-LILI, HI-LO

Words by HELEN DEUTSCH
Music by BRONISLAU KAPER

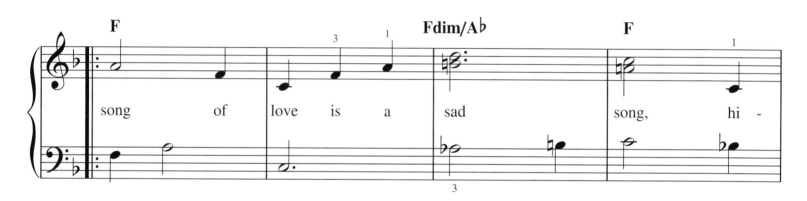

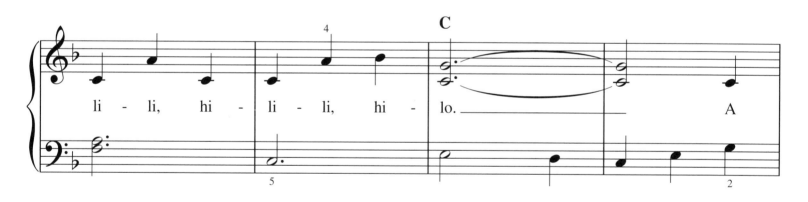

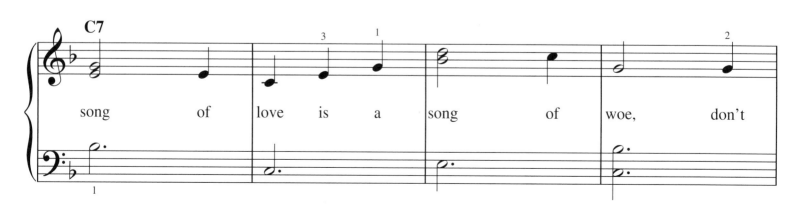

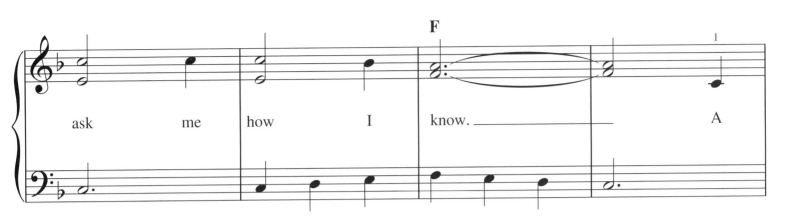

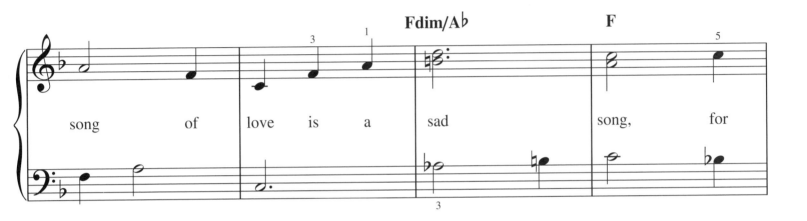

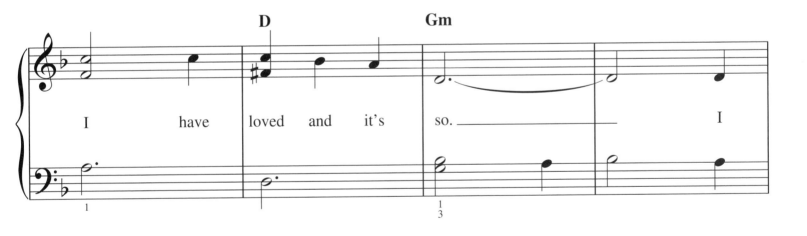

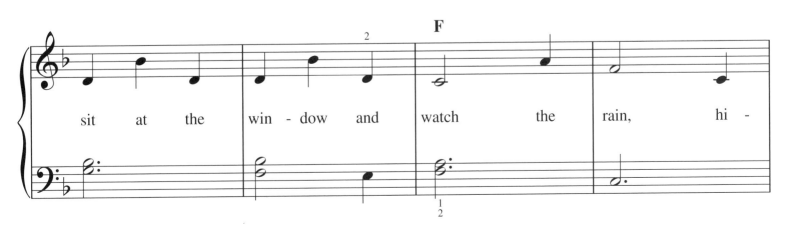

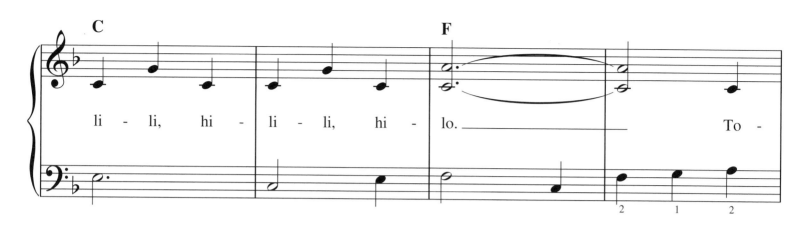

li - li, hi - li - li, hi - lo. _____ To -

mor - row I'll prob - a - bly love a - gain, hi -

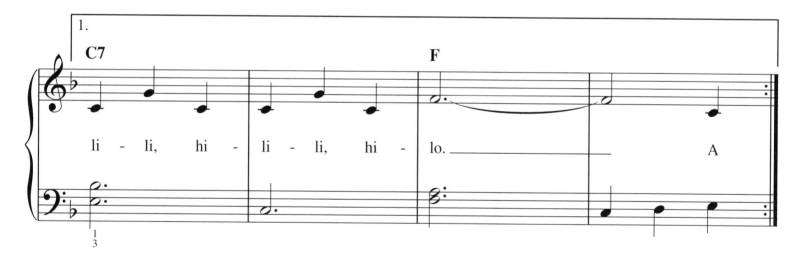

1.

li - li, hi - li - li, hi - lo. _____ A

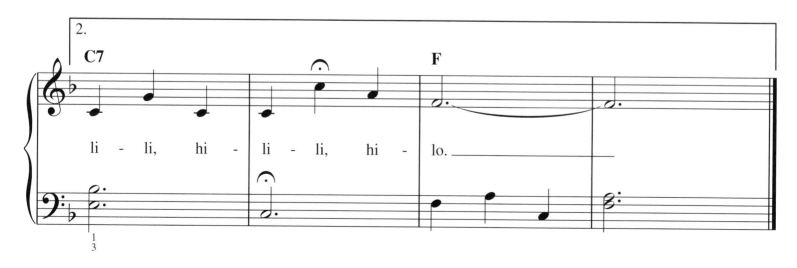

2.

li - li, hi - li - li, hi - lo. _____

THE HOKEY POKEY

Words and Music by CHARLES P. MACAK,
TAFFT BAKER and LARRY LaPRISE

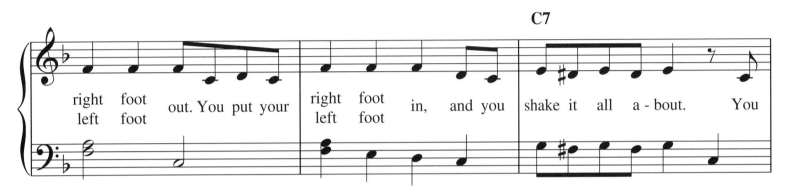

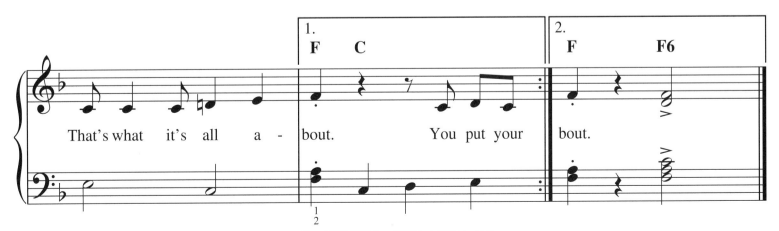

I'M AN OLD COWHAND
(From the Rio Grande)

Words and Music by
JOHNNY MERCER

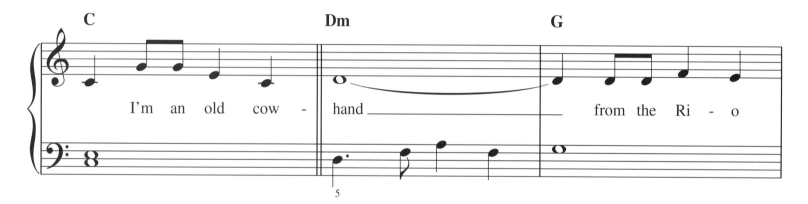

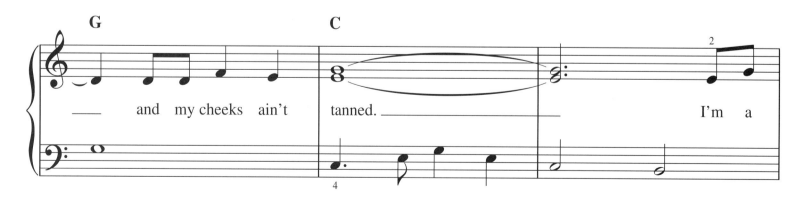

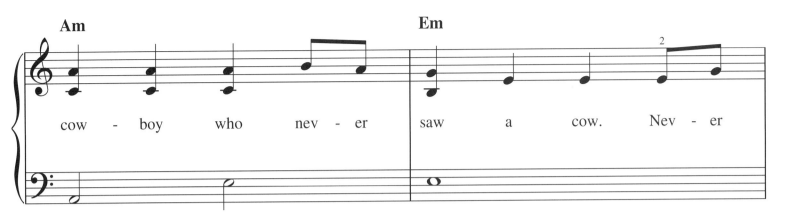

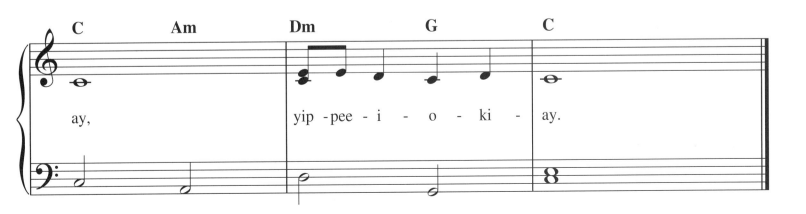

IF I ONLY HAD A BRAIN
from THE WIZARD OF OZ

Lyrics by E.Y. "YIP" HARBURG
Music by HAROLD ARLEN

trou-ble or in pain.
gard-ing love and art.
fate I don't de-serve.

With the | thoughts I'd be think-in' I could
I'd be | friends with the spar-rows and the
But I | could show my prow-ess, be a

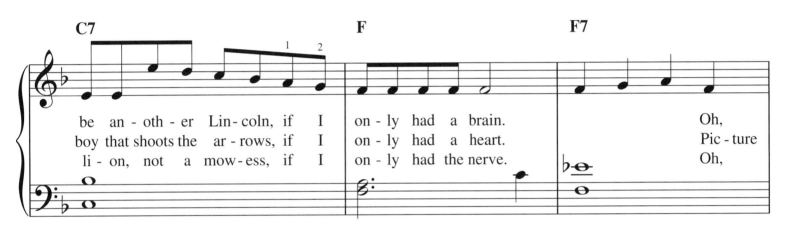

be an-oth-er Lin-coln, if I | on-ly had a brain. | Oh,
boy that shoots the ar-rows, if I | on-ly had a heart. | Pic-ture
li-on, not a mow-ess, if I | on-ly had the nerve. | Oh,

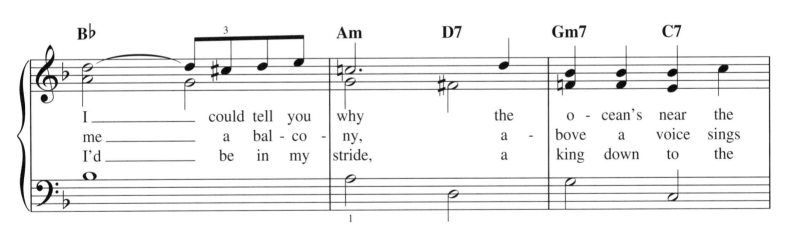

I _____ could tell you | why | the | o-cean's near the
me _____ a bal-co-|ny, | a-|bove a voice sings
I'd _____ be in my | stride, | a | king down to the

shore. | I could | think of things I | nev-er thunk be-|fore, | and then I'd
low, | "Where-fore | art thou, Ro-me-|o?" | I hear a
core. | Oh, I'd | roar the way I | nev-er roared be-|fore, | and then I'd

sit　　　　and think some | more.　　How | I would | not be just a nuff-in'　　my
beat.　　　　How | sweet!　　Just to | reg-is-ter e-mo-tion,
rrrwoof,　　　and roar some | more.　　I would | show the di-no-sau-rus　who's

head all full of stuff-in'　my | heart all full of pain. | And per-
jeal-ous-y, de-vo-tion, and | real-ly feel the part, | I would
king a-round the for-res', a | king they bet-ter serve. | Why, with

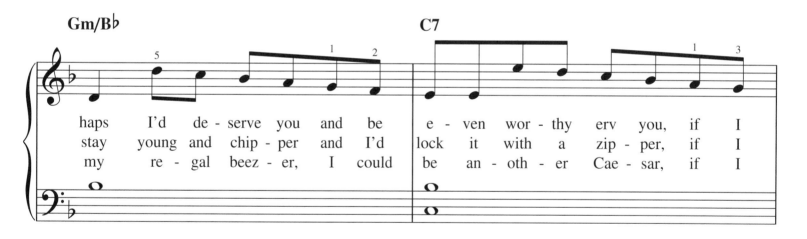

haps I'd de-serve you and be | e-ven wor-thy erv you, if I
stay young and chip-per and I'd | lock it with a zip-per, if I
my re-gal beez-er, I could | be an-oth-er Cae-sar, if I

on-ly had a brain. | When a
on-ly had a heart. | Life is
on-ly had the nerve.

OVER THE RAINBOW
from THE WIZARD OF OZ

Music by HAROLD ARLEN
Lyric by E.Y. "YIP" HARBURG

When all the clouds dark-en up the sky-way, there's a rain-bow high-way to be

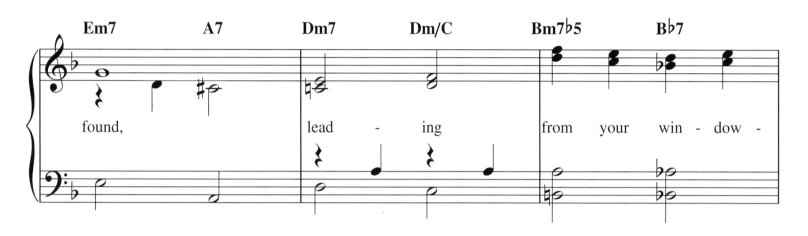

found, lead - ing from your win - dow -

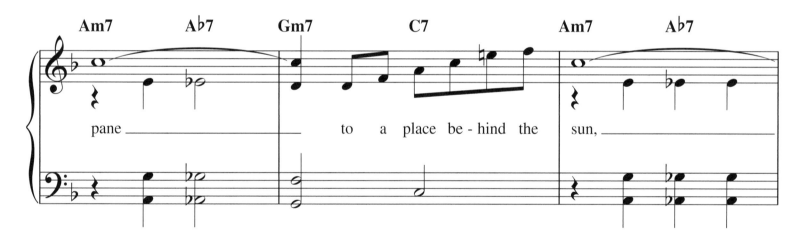

pane _____ to a place be-hind the sun, _____

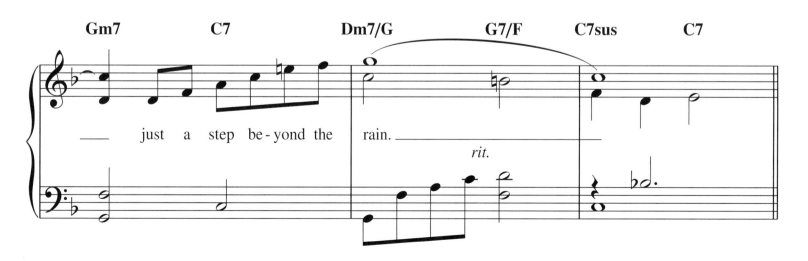

_____ just a step be-yond the rain. _____

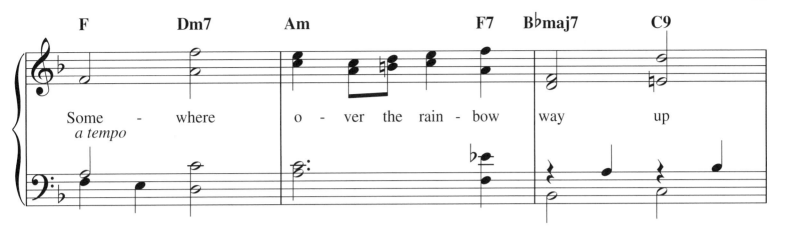

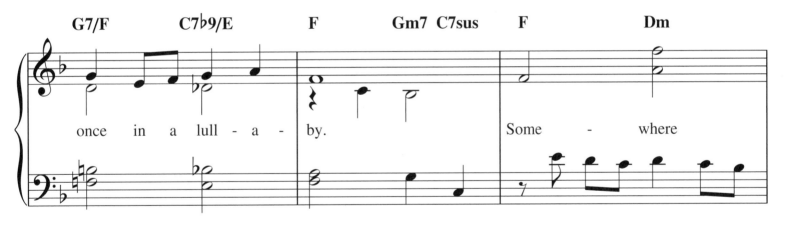

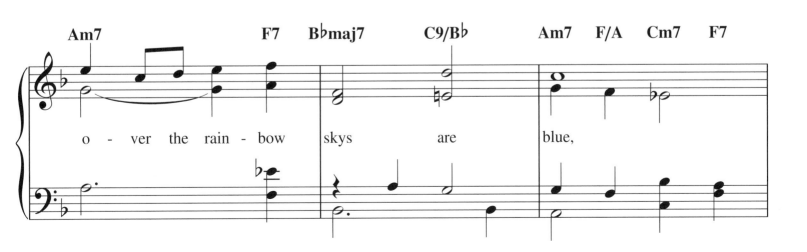

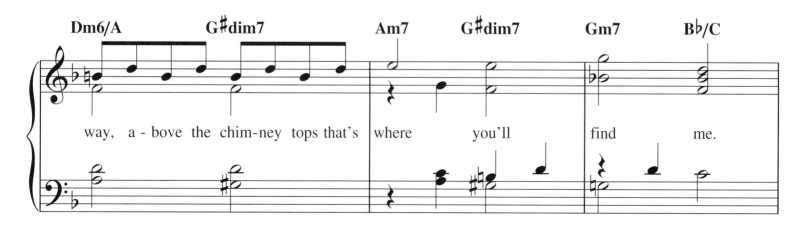

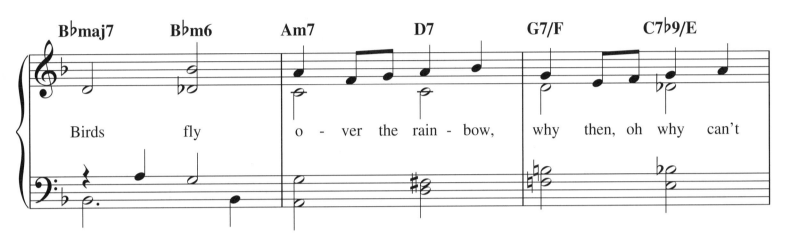

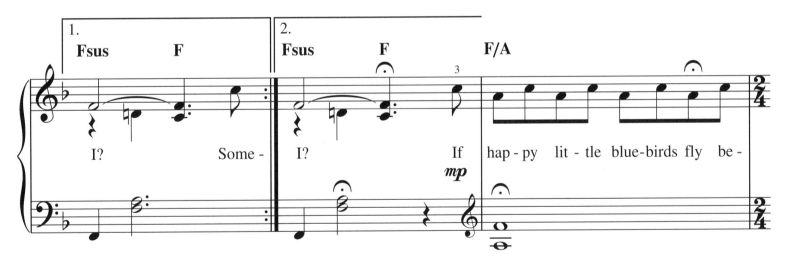

RAGTIME COWBOY JOE

Words and Music by LEWIS F. MUIR,
GRANT CLARKE and MAURICE ABRAHAMS

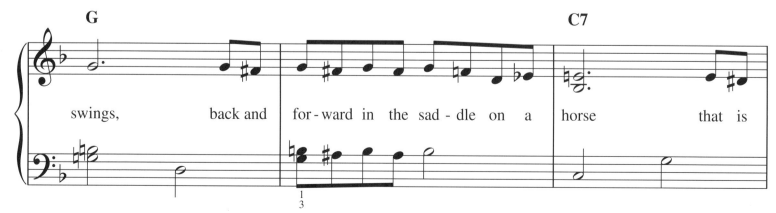

F **Dm7** **G** **C7**

syn-co-pat-ed gait-ed, and there's such a fun-ny me-ter to the sound of his re-peat-er, how they

F **G** **A7**

run when they hear that fel-low's guns, be-cause the West-ern folks all know, he's a

Dm **F/C** **G/B** **F/C** **C7**

high fa-lut-in', scoot-in', shoot-in', son of a gun from Ar-i-zo-na, Rag-time Cow-boy

1.
F

Joe. He al-ways

2.
G9 **C7** **Dm7** **G9 C7** **F**

oh, what a cow-boy, Rag-time Cow-boy Joe!

THE RIVER SEINE
(La Seine)

Words and Music by ALLAN ROBERTS
and ALAN HOLT
Original French Text by FLAVIEN MONOD
and GUY LaFARGE

Moderately

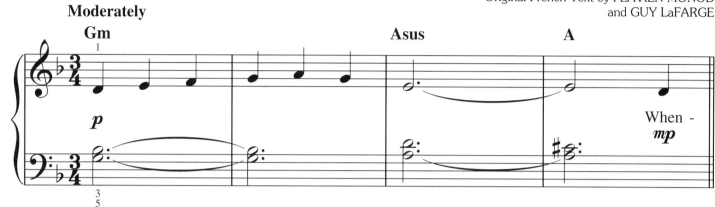

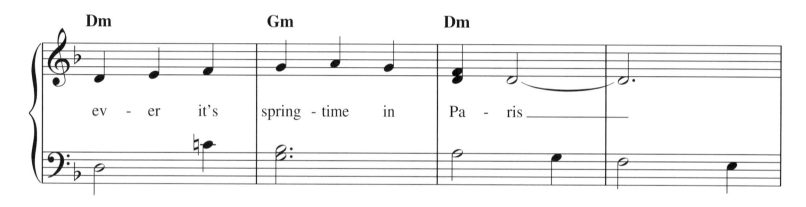

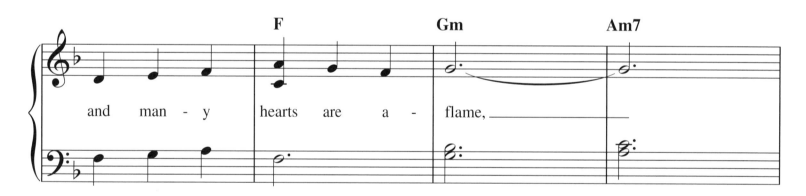

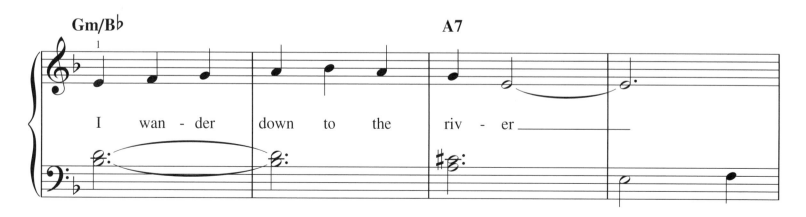

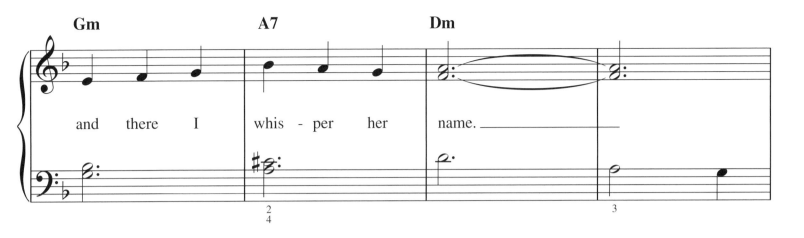

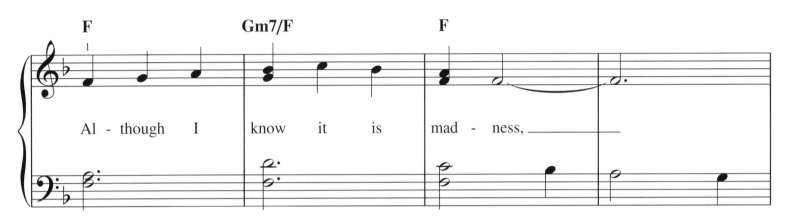

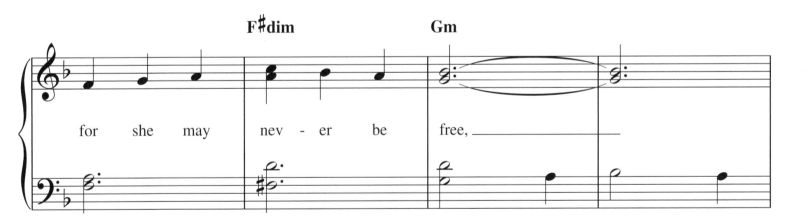

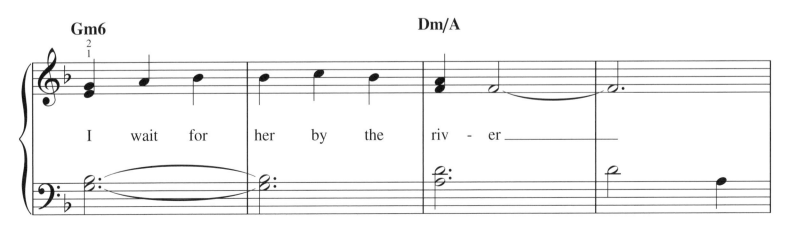

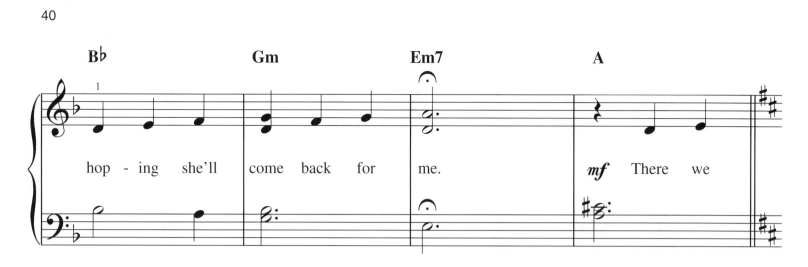

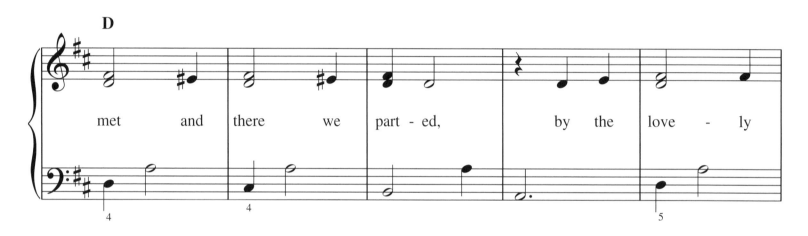

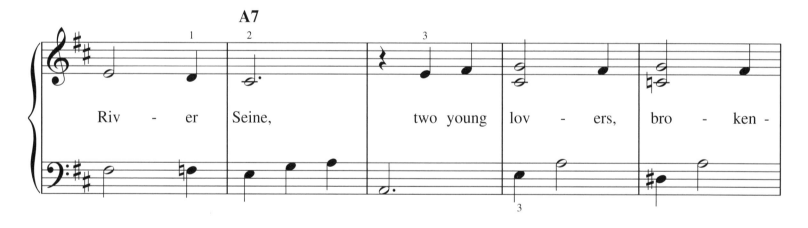

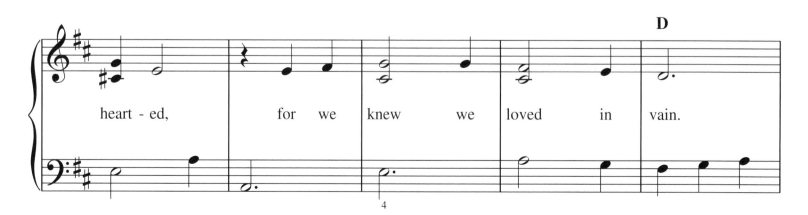

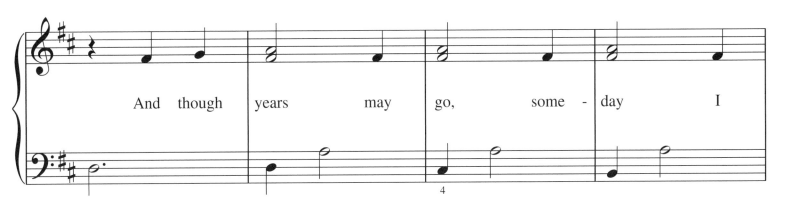

And though years may go, some-day I

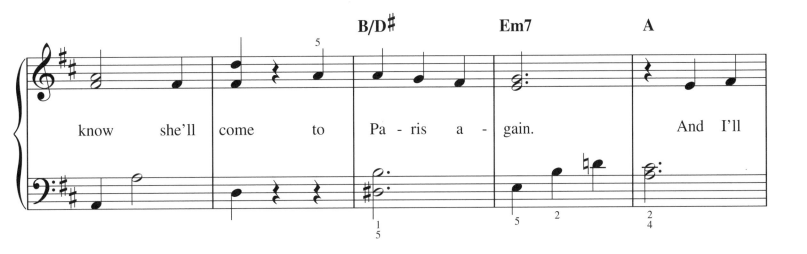

know she'll come to Pa - ris a - gain. And I'll

find her where I lost her, by the

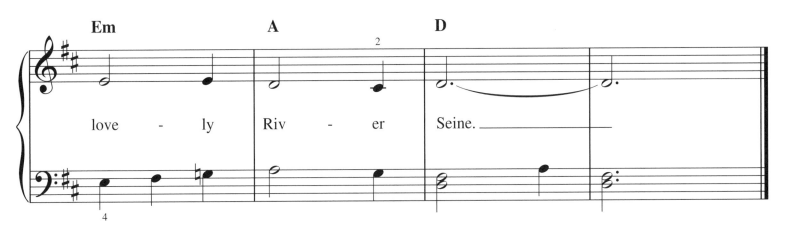

love - ly Riv - er Seine.

THE SYNCOPATED CLOCK

Music by LEROY ANDERSON
Words by MITCHELL PARISH

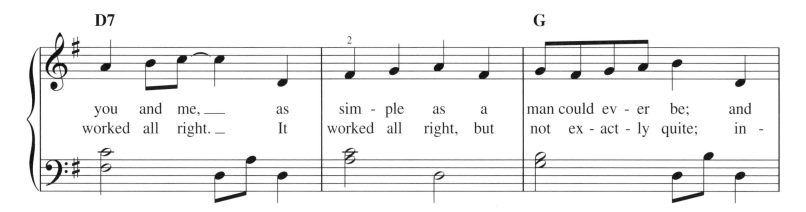

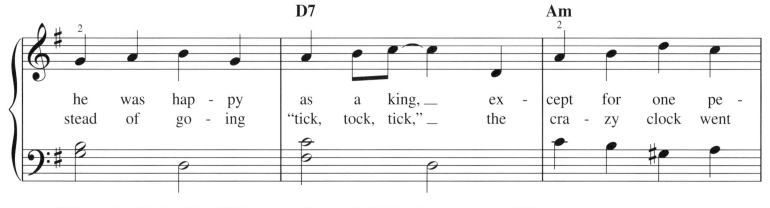

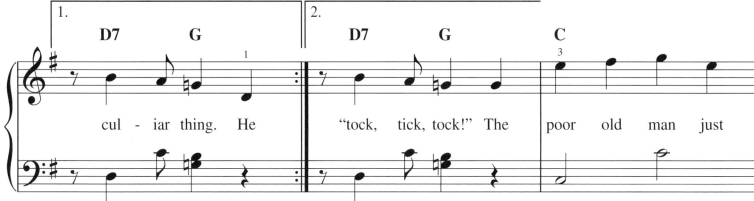

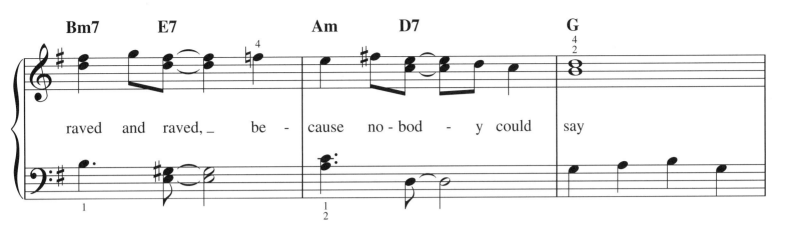

raved and raved, _ be - cause no - bod _ y could say

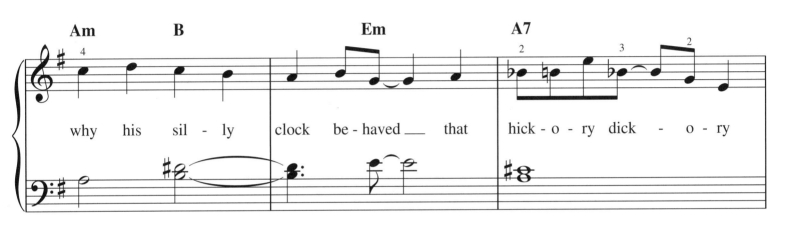

why his sil - ly clock be - haved ___ that hick - o - ry dick - o - ry

way. But now a fa - mous man is he. ___ He owns a pub - lic

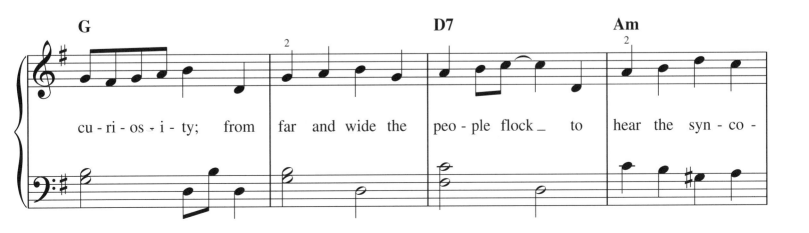

cu - ri - os - i - ty; from far and wide the peo - ple flock _ to hear the syn - co -

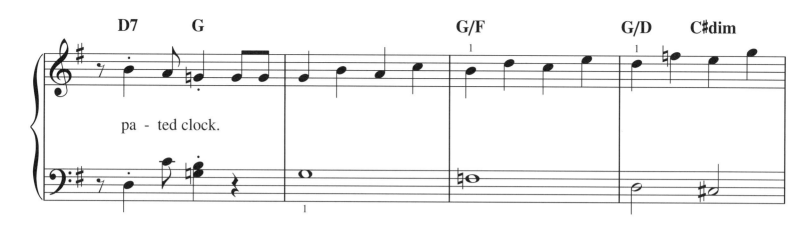

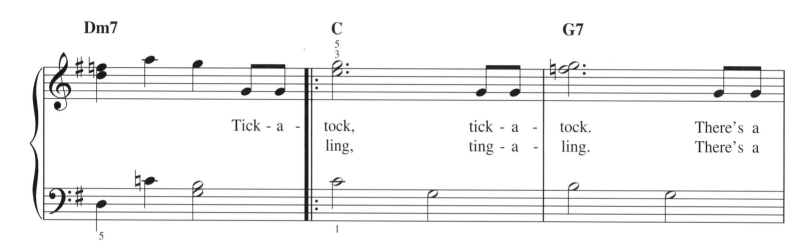

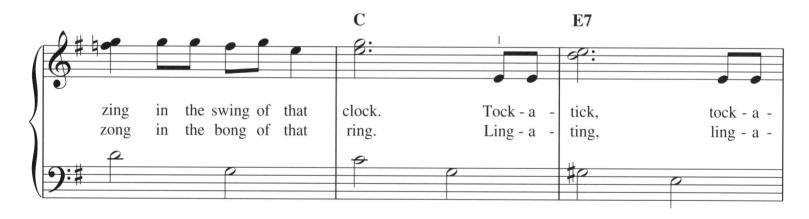

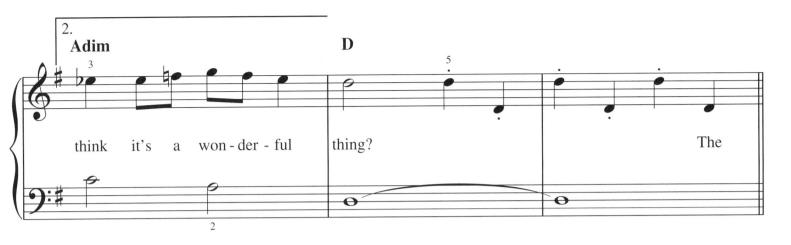

think it's a won-der-ful thing? The

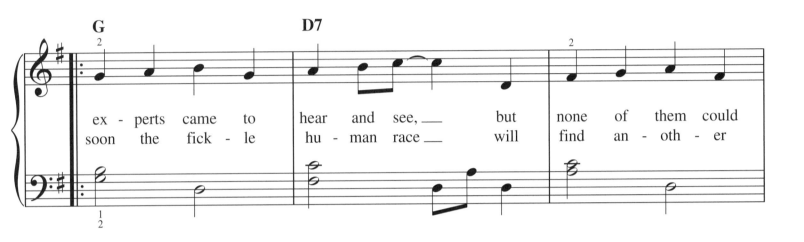

ex - perts came to hear and see, ___ but none of them could
soon the fick - le hu - man race ___ will find an - oth - er

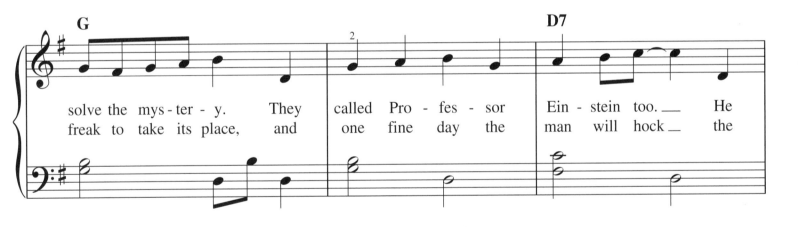

solve the mys - ter - y. They called Pro - fes - sor Ein - stein too. ___ He
freak to take its place, and one fine day the man will hock ___ the

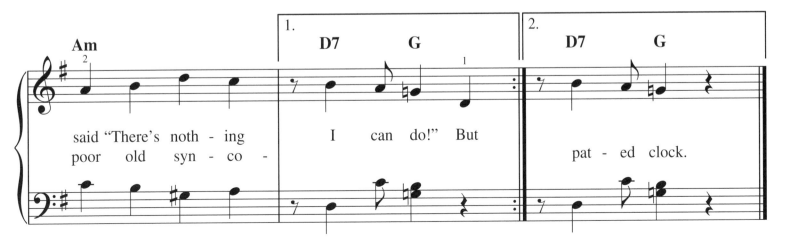

said "There's noth - ing I can do!" But
poor old syn - co - pat - ed clock.

THIS LAND IS YOUR LAND

Words and Music by
WOODY GUTHRIE

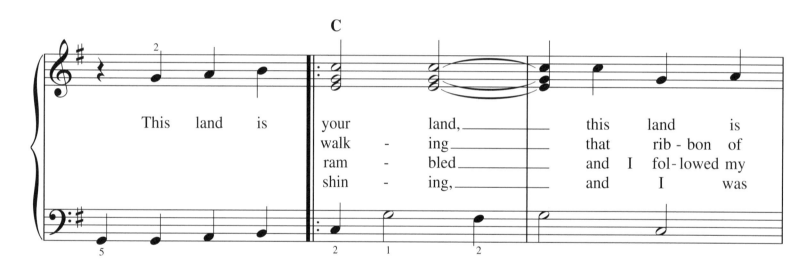

This land is | your land,_____ | this land is
walk - ing_____ | that rib - bon of
ram - bled_____ | and I fol-lowed my
shin - ing,_____ | and I was

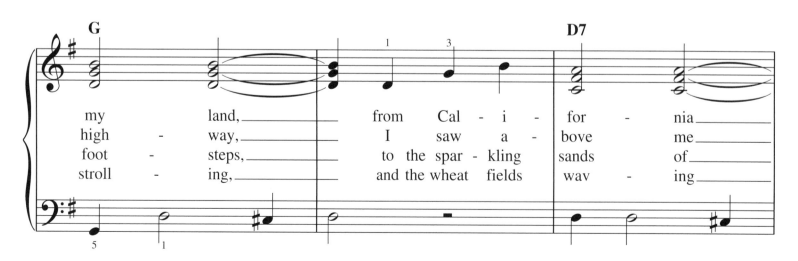

my land,_____ | from Cal - i - for - nia_____
high - way,_____ | I saw a - bove me_____
foot - steps,_____ | to the spar - kling sands of_____
stroll - ing,_____ | and the wheat fields wav - ing_____

WE'RE OFF TO SEE THE WIZARD

Lyrics by E.Y. "YIP" HARBURG
Music by HAROLD ARLEN

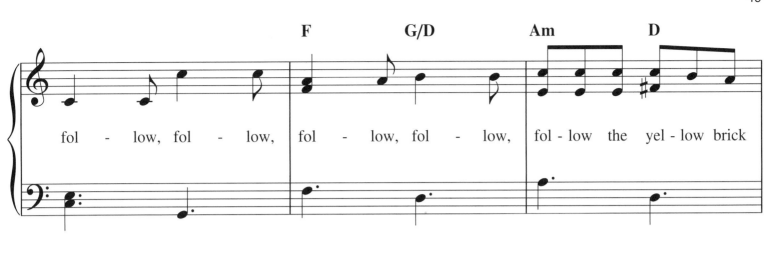

fol - low, fol - low, fol - low, fol - low, fol - low the yel - low brick

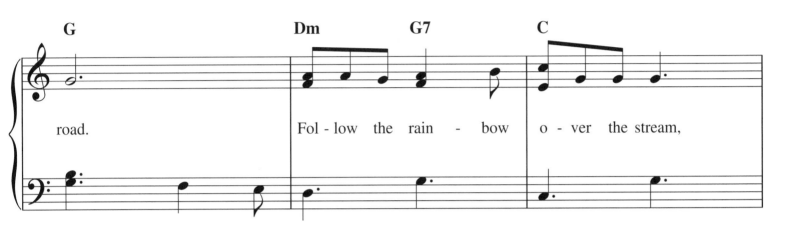

road. Fol - low the rain - bow o - ver the stream,

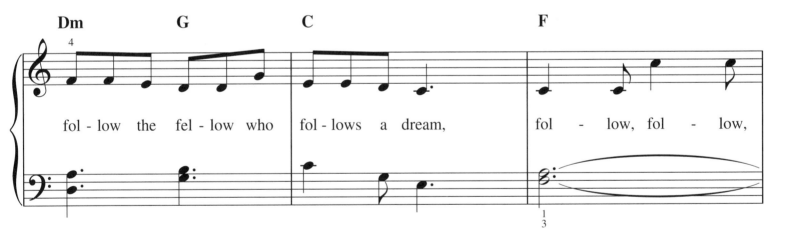

fol - low the fel - low who fol - lows a dream, fol - low, fol - low,

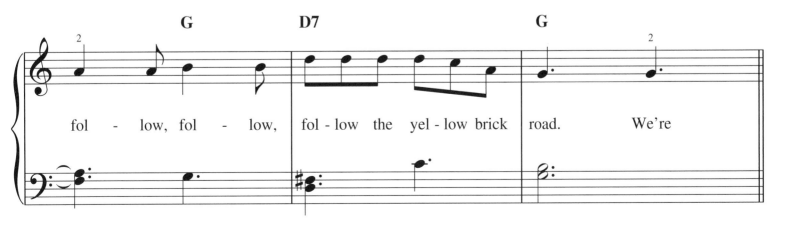

fol - low, fol - low, fol - low the yel - low brick road. We're

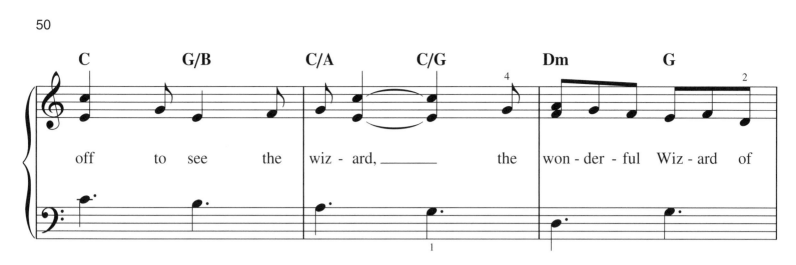

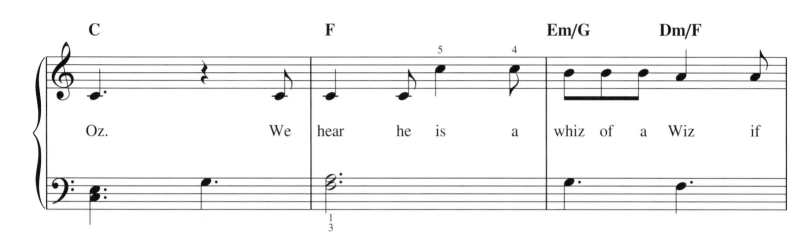

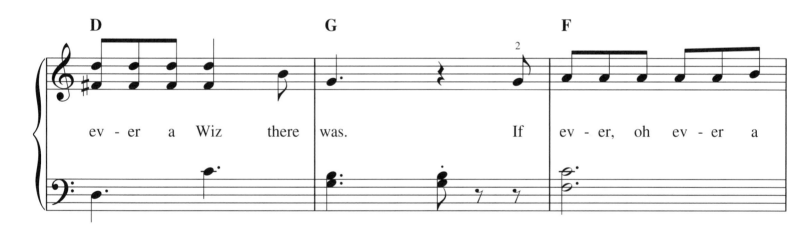

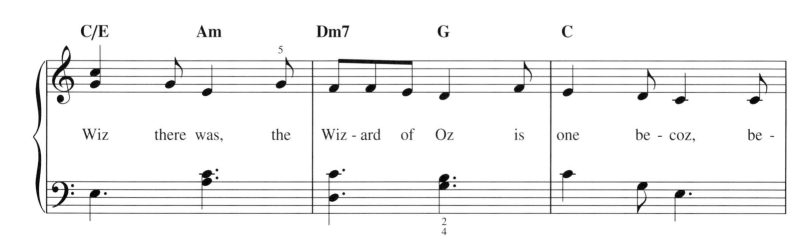

coz,   be - coz,   be - coz,   be - coz,   be - coz,

be - coz of the won-der-ful   things   he does.

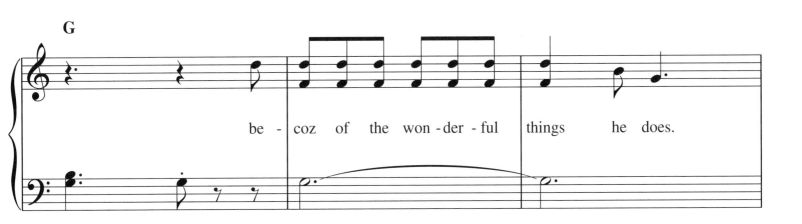

We're   off   to   see   the

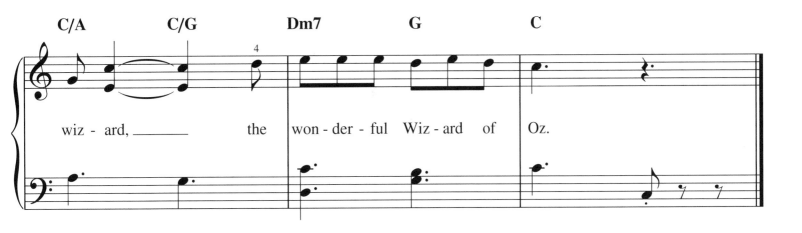

wiz - ard, _____   the   won-der-ful Wiz-ard of   Oz.

WHEN I GROW TOO OLD TO DREAM

Lyrics by OSCAR HAMMERSTEIN II
Music by SIGMUND ROMBERG

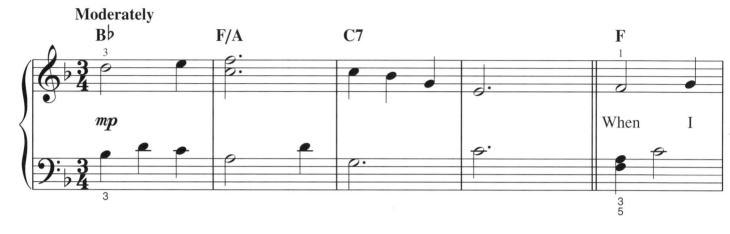

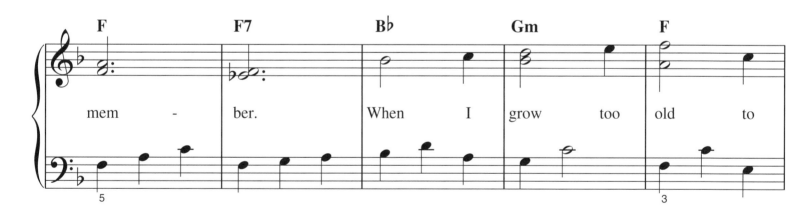

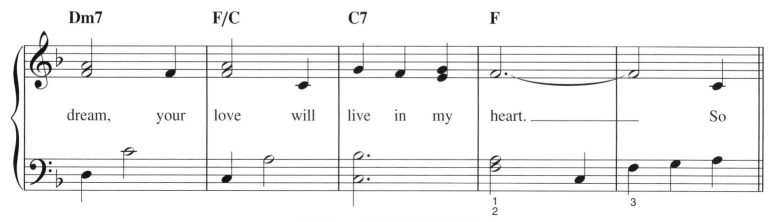

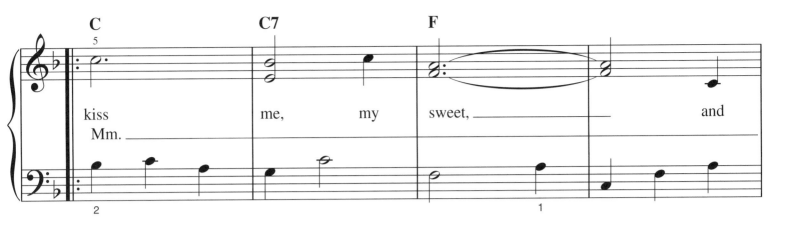

kiss me, my sweet, _____ and
Mm. _____

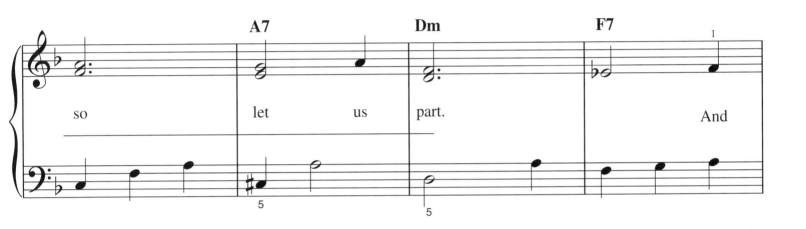

so let us part. And

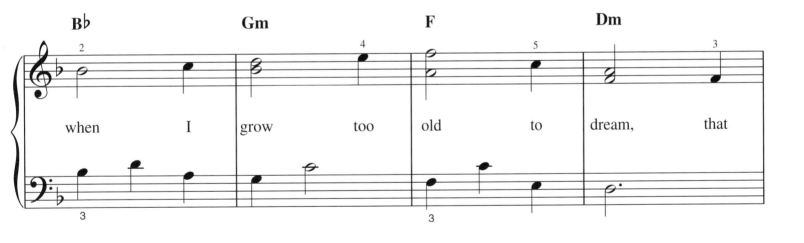

when I grow too old to dream, that

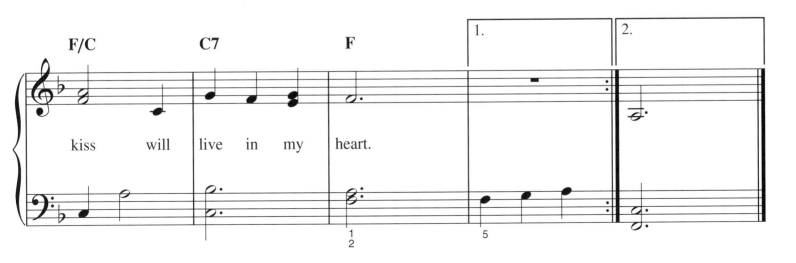

kiss will live in my heart.

1.

2.

SING
from SESAME STREET

Words and Music by
JOE RAPOSO

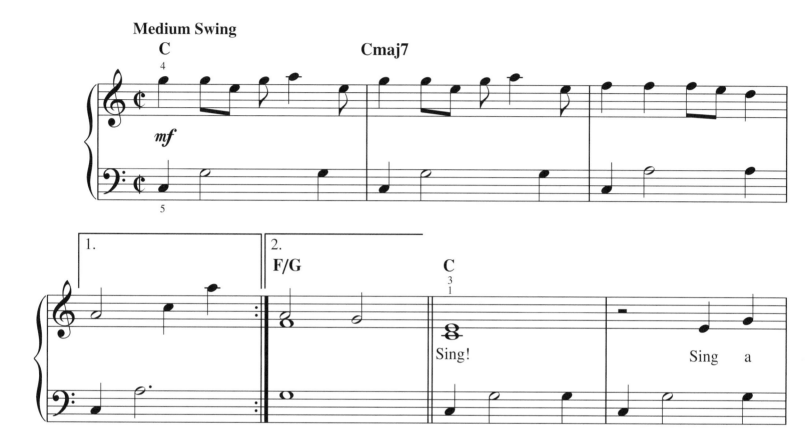

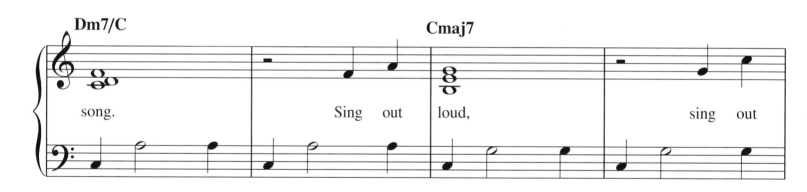

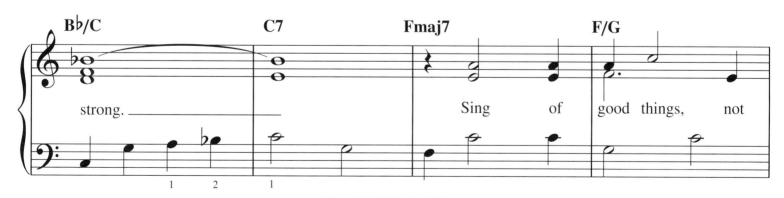

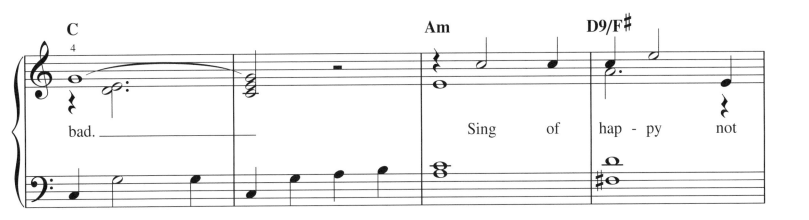

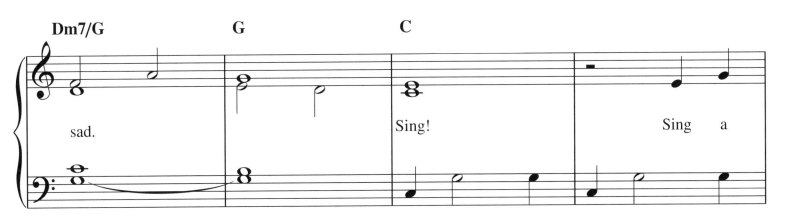

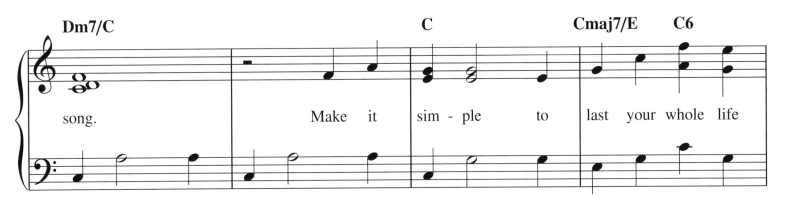

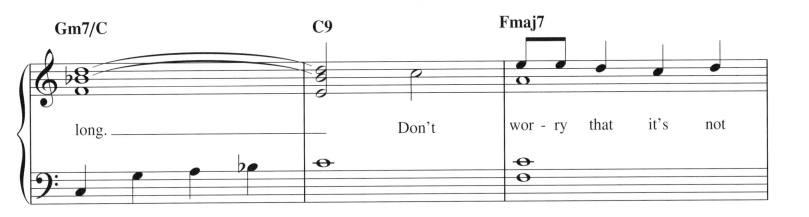

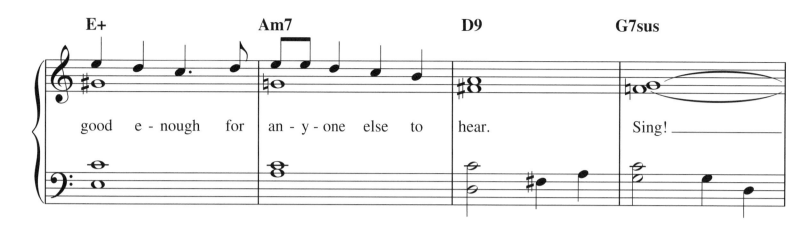

E+ | **Am7** | **D9** | **G7sus**

good e - nough for an - y - one else to hear. Sing! _____

G7 | **C**

— Sing a song. La la do la da, la

Cmaj7 | **Fmaj7/C** | **F/G** | **C**

da la do la da, la da da la do la da. La la do la da, la

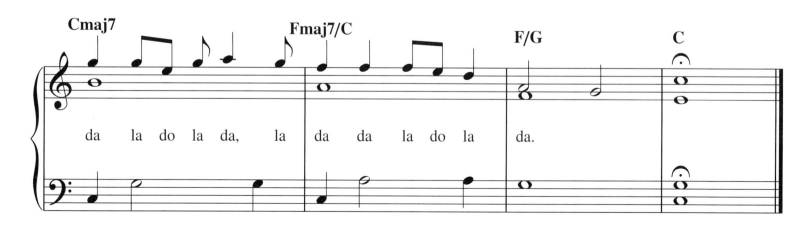

Cmaj7 | **Fmaj7/C** | **F/G** | **C**

da la do la da, la da da la do la da.